LA FAMILIA ROCHA

Libro 2: Redolfo Orosco

Written by Edward Lee Rocha
Illustrated by Angie Hurshman

For Dad

Writing: Edward Lee Rocha

Art and Layout: Angie Hurshman

Copyright © Rola Corporation 2021

ISBN: 9781087951201

Redolfo es mexicano-americano y es de Tejas. Es tejano. Él tiene 25 años.

Es un trabajador en la granja pero le gustaría ser carpintero. Él quiere ser carpintero.

Tejano
Texan

Trabajador
Worker

Gustaría
Would like

Carpintero
Carpenter

1

Él es muy simpático y cómico.
Le gusta bailar y correr.
Baila muy bien y corre rápido.
Es moreno y tiene pelo negro.
Su nombre se deletrea:
R-E-D-O-L-F-O.

Simpático	Cómico	Bailar	Moreno
Nice	Funny	To Dance	Tan

Redolfo tiene muchos amigos.

Su mejor amigo, Bruster, es policía, y su amigo, Alfredo, es peluquero.

Mejor Amigo
Best Friend

Policía
Police officer

Peluquero
Barber

Él tiene muchas amigas también.
Su amiga, Bárbara, es cartera,
y su amiga, Camila, es abogada.
Redolfo trabaja con una mujer
que se llama María Guadalupe.

Muchas	**Cartera**	**Abogada**	**Mujer**
Many	Mail Carrier	Lawyer	Woman

En la granja, él ayuda
a sus compañeros.

Él cultiva vegetales como
maíz y pepino. Él maneja
una camioneta roja
y limpia el granero.

Ayuda	Compañeros	Maíz	Pepino	Camioneta	Granero
Helps	Coworkers	Corn	Cucumber	Truck	Barn

Él no va a la escuela, pero le gusta estudiar.
Le gustan los libros.

Le gusta estudiar verbos como
hablar, preguntar, correr,
comer, escribir, y construir.
Habla inglés y español.

Preguntar	Correr	Comer	Escribir	Construir
To Ask	To Run	To Eat	To Write	To Build

Redolfo tiene una familia cariñosa. Tiene una mamá.
Ella se llama Suzy y es seria y baja.
Ella cocina tortillas deliciosas.
Su padrastro se llama Julio y es muy alto.
Su hermana es Beatriz y es vendedora.

Mamá	Seria	Padrastro	Vendedora	
Mom	Serious	Stepfather	Salesperson	7

Redolfo quiere ser carpintero. Él practica cuando no trabaja.
Él pinta su casa. Le gusta construir cosas también.

$$a^2$$
$$+b^2$$
$$=c^2$$

Cuando construye cosas, tiene que usar matemáticas.
Le gustan las matemáticas.

Practica	Pinta	Usar	Matemáticas
Practices	Paints	To Use	Math

Le gusta pintar,
pero NO QUIERE ser pintor.

Le gusta cocinar comida
mexicana como arroz con frijoles,
pero NO QUIERE ser cocinero.

¡QUIERE SER CARPINTERO!

Pintor
Painter

Arroz
Rice

Frijoles
Beans

Cocinero
Cook

¡Ayúdame!
Help me!

¿Quién es Redolfo?
Who is Redolfo?

¿Dónde trabaja?
Where does he work?

¿Cómo se llaman sus amigos?
What are his friends' names?

¿Cómo es Redolfo?
What is Redolfo like?

¿Qué vegetales cultiva Redolfo en la granja?
What vegetables does Redolfo grow on the farm?

¿Qué quiere ser Redolfo?
What does Redolfo want to be?

11

Thanks for reading!
If you would like to listen to the
audio of this book or purchase other
books in the series, please visit:
LaFamiliaRocha.com

This book is a creation of
Rola Corporation and was written by
Edward Lee Rocha.
Picture Credits: Angie Hurshman

Vocabulario

Tejano	Texan		Camioneta	Truck
Trabajador	Worker		Granero	Barn
Gustaría	Would Like		Preguntar	To Ask
Carpintero	Carpenter		Correr	To Run
Simpático	Nice		Comer	To Eat
Cómico	Funny		Escribir	To Write
Bailar	To Dance		Construir	To Build
Moreno	Tan		Mamá	Mom
Mejor Amigo	Best Friend		Seria	Serious
Policía	Police Officer		Padrastro	Stepfather
Peluquero	Barber		Vendedora	Salesperson
Muchas	Many		Practica	Practices
Cartera	Mail Carrier		Pinta	Paints
Abogada	Lawyer		Usar	To Use
Mujer	Woman		Matemáticas	Math
Ayuda	Helps		Pintor	Painter
Compañeros	Coworkers		Arroz	Rice
Maíz	Corn		Frijoles	Beans
Pepino	Cucumber		Cocinero	Cook

Edward Rocha is the founder and President of Rola Corporation and director of Rola Languages. Ed is fluent in English and Spanish and a student of French, Portuguese, and Mandarin with nearly 20 years of language teaching experience. After privately tutoring Spanish for many years and living abroad in Argentina and Spain, he fell in love with the idea of a language school, and as an avid entrepreneur and language and communications specialist, Ed was determined to build such a community in Boston. He formalized his teaching method and thus, Rola Languages was born in 2008.

Angie Hurshman is an illustrator determined to fill life with color. She grew up in the eccentric culture of Austin, TX. Her hometown's liveliness, and the styles of the mid century during which Austin rapidly grew, exist in her illustrations. Seeing the wonder and fun in life is something she wanted to share, and in addition to the desire to take flight, she enrolled at the New Hampshire Institute of Art, and earned a BFA in Illustration in 2017. She now lives in New England with her husband, son, and two cats. These days her toddler helps inspire her art with a relived sense of childlike wonder!

About the Series:

La Familia Rocha series is an introductory Spanish series for children language learners. The goal is to help students practice Spanish, while having fun and learning vocabulary. Book 2, Redolfo Orosco, is the second installment in the six-part series and introduces Redolfo. After learning about María in book 1, now readers will learn all about Redolfo and his life! Continue on your Spanish journey and learn about María, Redolfo, and how they fell in love! Each book in the series will be progressive in nature. Readers will learn more Spanish and about the characters in the series. This children's book is ideal for parents and children alike. At the bottom of each page, students and parents can find key Spanish vocabulary words and their English translations. Stay tuned for the next La Familia Rocha adventure!

CPSIA information can be obtained
at www.ICGtesting.com
Printed in the USA
BVHW021122220621
610209BV00010B/403